The FIRST THANKSGIVING

By Kathleen Connors

Gareth Stevens
Publishing

Please visit our website, www.garethstevens.com. For a free color catalog of all our high-quality books, call toll free 1-800-542-2595 or fax 1-877-542-2596.

Library of Congress Cataloging-in-Publication Data

Connors, Kathleen.
The first Thanksgiving / by Kathleen Connors.
 p. cm. — (What you didn't know about history)
Includes index.
ISBN 978-1-4824-0582-8 (pbk.)
ISBN 978-1-4824-0584-2 (6-pack)
ISBN 978-1-4824-0581-1 (library binding)
1. Thanksgiving Day — Juvenile literature. 2. Pilgrims (New Plymouth Colony) — Juvenile literature. 3. Massachusetts — History — New Plymouth, 1620-1691 — Juvenile literature. I. Connors, Kathleen. II. Title.
GT4975.C66 2014
394.2649—dc23

First Edition

Published in 2014 by
Gareth Stevens Publishing
111 East 14th Street, Suite 349
New York, NY 10003

Copyright © 2014 Gareth Stevens Publishing

Designer: Andrea Davison-Bartolotta
Editor: Kristen Rajczak

Photo credits: Cover, p. 1 courtesy of the Library of Congress; p. 4 iStockphoto/Thinkstock; p. 5 American School/The Bridgeman Art Library/Getty Images; pp. 7, 15 Frederic Lewis/ Getty Images; p. 8 Interim Archives/Getty Images; p. 9 Lambert/Getty Images; p. 11 Antonio Gisbert/The Bridgeman Art Library/Getty Images; pp. 12, 13, 19 Kean Collection/ Getty Images; p. 17 Jenni A. Brownscombe/Wikimedia Commons; p. 20 Monkey Business Images/Shutterstock.com; p. 21 (turkey) iStockphoto/Thinkstock; p. 21 (pumpkin) Hemera/ Thinkstock; p. 21 (football) Stockbyte/Thinkstock.

Printed in the United States of America

CPSIA compliance information: Batch #CW14GS: For further information contact Gareth Stevens, New York, New York at 1-800-542-2595.

CONTENTS

Words in the glossary appear in **bold** type the first time they are used in the text.

A HAPPY HOLIDAY

Many Americans celebrate the fourth Thursday in November by watching football and eating a big meal with their family. This is the national holiday of Thanksgiving, a **tradition** linked to the Pilgrims and their early days in the **New World**.

But pictures showing the Pilgrims sitting down for a feast with their Native American friends are only partly right. Stories about this day often make it sound much nicer than it was. So, what was the first Thanksgiving *really* like?

modern Thanksgiving meal

The Pilgrims landed in North America in 1620. They soon met a Native American group called the Wampanoag.

Did You Know?

The Pilgrims were a mix of people who sailed from Europe to North America together in 1620. Some of them were interested in making a living in the colonies. Others were fleeing **persecution** for their religion, or faith.

FACT AND FICTION

In the fall of 1621, there was a feast in Plymouth, the colony founded by the Pilgrims. It likely lasted for 3 days and took place sometime between the end of September and the beginning of November.

However, calling this meal the "first Thanksgiving" is a little misleading. The Pilgrims didn't plan to start a yearly tradition. In fact, they were just continuing an English practice of offering a meal of thanksgiving for their good fortune! Similarly, the Wampanoag people "gave thanks" daily for what they had.

Did You Know?

The Wampanoag tribe lived in the area the Pilgrims made their home—now southeastern Massachusetts—for 12,000 years before settlers came.

Meals of thanksgiving became a tradition in the New England area, though there wasn't a set day called Thanksgiving until the 1800s.

WHAT DO WE KNOW?

While Pilgrims wear hats with buckles and Native Americans have feather headdresses in Thanksgiving decorations and pictures, many **details** like these have been invented over the years. Historians don't actually know much about that meal!

Most of the facts they do have come from two **sources**. In a letter, a man named Edward Winslow wrote about a great thanksgiving meal with the Wampanoag. William Bradford, one of the early leaders of Plymouth Colony, also wrote about it in a book.

Did You Know?

William Bradford's account of the first Thanksgiving was lost until 1854. So, the earliest beliefs about the meal came from Winslow's letter.

Edward Winslow

In paintings of the first Thanksgiving, the Pilgrims are often dressed in black and brown. In truth, they wore bright, cheerful clothing, too.

GIVING THANKS

The reason for the first Thanksgiving is in its name—the Pilgrims wanted to give thanks! It's often said the Pilgrims were thankful for a good harvest. But the feast **celebrated** much more than that. The first year in Plymouth, many colonists died of illness and hunger. Many lost hope their settlement would be successful. The 52 colonists left were **grateful** to be alive.

Historians know the Pilgrims celebrated another meal of thanksgiving in 1623. They were thankful for rain after 2 months without any.

Did You Know?

Days of thanksgiving were also celebrated in colonial Canada, even as far back as the 1580s. Today, Canada's Thanksgiving Day is the second Monday in October.

Thanksgiving meals were tied to Puritanism, the faith some Pilgrims followed. Prayers were often said at these meals.

11

 GUESTS

The meal we call the first Thanksgiving may have also been in celebration of an agreement between the Wampanoag and the Pilgrims. Winslow's letter mentions another reason the Native Americans may have come to Plymouth Colony. They heard gunshots!

A group of men from the colony were hunting in preparation for the feast. The Wampanoag heard the shooting and may have worried the colonists were going to attack. About 90 Wampanoag arrived at the colony, and, seeing that nothing was wrong, stayed for the feast!

Squanto

The first Thanksgiving marked a peaceful moment between the colonists and the Native Americans, though the two groups often attacked each other. Today, some Native Americans view Thanksgiving unfavorably because of this.

Did You Know?

The first Thanksgiving could have been a quiet affair since the Pilgrims and Wampanoag didn't speak the same language! Tisquantum, or Squanto, who had helped the settlers with their crops, acted as an **interpreter**.

THE MEAL

What do you make for Thanksgiving dinner? Turkey, stuffing, and mashed potatoes are some of the most common dishes served today—and none of those were at the first Thanksgiving!

The Pilgrims did serve "fowl," which could mean turkey. But it probably meant duck or goose, which were easier to hunt. The Wampanoag brought venison, or deer meat. Corn, shellfish, and fish were also probably part of the feast. There may have been grapes or plums, too.

Did You Know?

While it's possible that squash or pumpkin was eaten at the first Thanksgiving, pumpkin pie wasn't. The Pilgrims didn't even have an oven to bake one in!

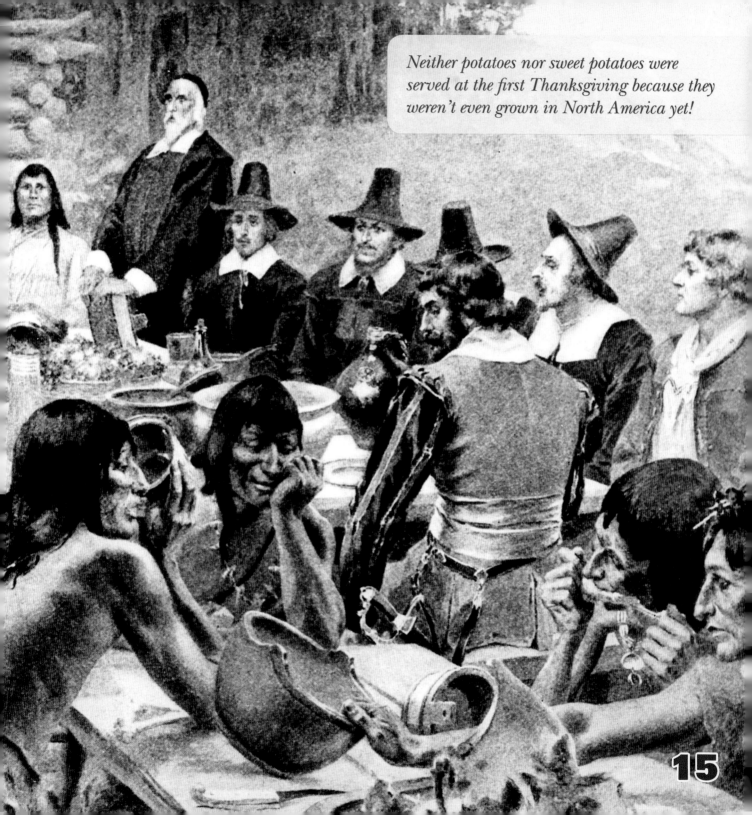

Neither potatoes nor sweet potatoes were served at the first Thanksgiving because they weren't even grown in North America yet!

FUN AND GAMES

The first Thanksgiving was a party! During the 3 days of the feast, the Pilgrims and Wampanoag danced and sang. They played ball games and ran races.

Do you set the table especially nice for Thanksgiving? The Pilgrims didn't! Not many buildings had been constructed yet, and many people ate outside. They sat on barrels—or on the ground—and likely held their plates in their lap. It wasn't a very formal affair.

Did You Know?
The first national day of thanksgiving was declared in 1777.

The Pilgrims didn't play football on Thanksgiving, but they still had lots of fun!

A MODERN MYTH

Our modern Thanksgiving was largely shaped during the 1800s. Turkey and big family dinners were already Thanksgiving traditions, though—just like today!

The **myth** of the "first" Thanksgiving began in 1841, when a book by historian Alexander Young noted that the feast in Edward Winslow's letter was the first Thanksgiving. Young also drew attention to the Pilgrim and Wampanoag roles in the 1621 feast. During the 1800s, it was more common to see paintings of colonists and Native Americans fighting than having dinner together.

Did You Know?

A magazine editor named Sarah Josepha Hale helped shape the myth of the first Thanksgiving, too. She printed stories and meal ideas for Thanksgiving, and tried to make it a national holiday.

During the early 1800s, Congress declared a few days of thanksgiving, but it wasn't yet a yearly holiday.

19

A TABLE FOR MANY

Abraham Lincoln declared Thanksgiving a national holiday in 1863. During the early 1900s, it helped Americans feel **united** as many **immigrants** came to the United States. All people, no matter where they came from, could celebrate it.

The Pilgrims and Native Americans who gave thanks together in 1621 didn't know they were part of the first Thanksgiving. And much of what is said about them isn't true. But their myth continues to bring our country together!

Did You Know?

George Washington, John Adams, and James Madison all proclaimed days of thanksgiving after events they thought Americans should be thankful for, such as the end of a war.

Truth About Thanksgiving Traditions

- Benjamin Franklin thought the wild turkey would be a more fitting national bird than the bald eagle. In 1784, Franklin wrote that the turkey was "a much more respectable bird."

- Yale and Princeton began the tradition of Thanksgiving Day football games in 1876. The National Football League held its first Thanksgiving game in 1934. The Detroit Lions played the Chicago Bears.

- The first Thanksgiving Day parade was put on in Philadelphia, Pennsylvania, by Gimbel's department store in 1920. Macy's Thanksgiving Day parade started in 1924.

- In 2005, the New Bremen Giant Pumpkin Growers in Ohio baked one of the largest pumpkin pies ever. It weighed more than 2,000 pounds (908 kg)!

LOSSARY

celebrate: to honor with special activities

detail: a small part

grateful: thankful

immigrant: one who comes to a new country to settle there

interpreter: a person who tells the meaning of things said in another language

myth: a legend or story

New World: the name colonists and explorers used to describe the Americas

persecution: making a group of people suffer cruel or unfair treatment

source: something that supplies information, such as a book

tradition: a long-practiced way of doing something

united: the state of being one

*F*OR MORE INFORMATION

Books

Gunderson, Jessica. *Thanksgiving Then and Now.* Mankato, MN: Picture Window Books, 2011.

Smith, Andrea P. *The First Thanksgiving.* New York, NY: PowerKids Press, 2012.

Websites

The First Thanksgiving
www.scholastic.com/scholastic_thanksgiving/
Watch videos, read historic letters, and even take a virtual trip around Plimouth Plantation on this website.

Thanksgiving Interactive: You Are the Historian
www.plimoth.org/learn/MRL/interact/thanksgiving-interactive-you-are-historian
Use Plimoth Plantation's interactive website to learn more about the first Thanksgiving.

$\mathcal{I}$NDEX